LONDON TROLLEYBUSES
a second album in black & white

Mick Webber

Capital Transport

Published by Capital Transport Publishing
www.capitaltransport.com

ISBN 978 1 85414 445 4

Printed by Parksons Graphics

An N1 class vehicle on loan from Bow to Ilford works the 691 in Barkingside High Street. 1614 was licensed in November 1939, and moved across to Stonebridge in 1959, where it remained until January 1962 when it was withdrawn for scrap. The 691 was very much a local route with a journey time of only 25 minutes. *John Wills*

Back cover: In the last days of London trolleybus operation in Kingston, L3 1417 is picking up passengers In London Road outside a once familiar High Street name, as it works a short to Malden on the 604. This would be the last of all London trolleybus routes on 8/9th May 1962. *John Wills*

INTRODUCTION

It was in 2009 that I sat down to write the introduction to the first London trolleybus black and white album. That book took the story of the London trolleybus from its inception in 1931 until 1950. The tram and trolleybus department of London Transport had always been run separately from the Central buses, but on 12th July 1950, the two were merged under the banner of Central Road Services. Until that point, trolleybus depots had no operational codes like central bus garages, and the vehicles just carried a running number plate. That all changed, and depots were coded after the merger, although Wandsworth vehicles never carried the code as they were withdrawn along with the trams, at the end of September. Several depots and bus garages shared the same name, and so to avoid confusion, six trolleybus depots were renamed, Sutton to Carshalton, Hendon to Colindale, Hackney to Clapton, Holloway to Highgate, Hounslow to Isleworth and Leyton to Lea Bridge. The fate of the trams had already been decided at this point, and within a few years, after much deliberation, the trolleybus system, it was decided, would be abandoned too.

The decade of the nineteen fifties was a quiet time for the fleet, and apart from the delivery of the second batch of Q1s, and the end of the Diddlers and prototype vehicles, services carried on as normal. The first major withdrawals commenced with a batch of 50 vehicles being sold for scrap to Thomson's of Cardiff, and from March 1956, many more went to Birds of Stratford upon Avon. The story of the conversion programme from March 1959 until May 1962 has been well documented elsewhere. The photographs chosen reflect the street scenes of the 1950s, and the rise in car ownership that enticed people away from public transport.

Most of the views in this album are previously unpublished, but no apology is made for reusing some where the larger page size of this book does justice to photos that have been used elsewhere at a smaller size.

I have to acknowledge Ken Blacker's two-volume definitive history of the London Trolleybus, also published by Capital Transport, and thank many for the use of their photographs for this book, which covers the period from October 1950 until May 1962. My thanks go to Tony Beard and the 2RT2 Bus Preservation Group for the use of the excellent collections of Norman Rayfield, Denis Battams and Sid Hagerty, and also to Alan Cross, Peter Horner, Jim Hawkins and Robin Newell for their help and encouragement.

Mick Webber

The two prototype trolleybuses built by London Transport were 62 and 63. No 62 was the forerunner of the large six-wheel fleet that followed. It was withdrawn in 1952, and is pictured here at Aldgate just before the merging of the tram and trolleybus department with Central buses, hence the single running number plate at waist level.
Mick Webber Collection

K2 class 1198 is leaving Commercial Street and is about to turn right into Shoreditch High Street on route 647. The impressive structure of Bishopsgate Goods Station forms the backdrop. The side profile of the standard London trolleybus is well illustrated here and this vehicle, having been delivered in November 1938, lasted until July 1961.

No 63, the only two-axle trolleybus in the London Transport fleet was originally operated from Fulwell, but was transferred to Hounslow during October 1948. Designed as a 60-seater prototype for London Transport's lighter routes, it was downseated to 58 before the war and the busy 657 was hardly the best place for it. Its service days ended in June 1952 and it is seen stored here at Fulwell awaiting sale to Thomson of Cardiff in February 1954. *John Gillham*

The London United Tramways operated trolleybuses 1-60, known as Diddlers, from their depot at Fulwell. The company experimented with a new more modern trolleybus, and the vehicle that became No 61, was constructed by AEC with centre entrance bodywork by the LGOC. It was first shown to the press in February 1933, but it did not enter service until July. This upper saloon view was taken in October 1952 after withdrawal. *John Gillham*

Trolleybus 98 had its body destroyed at Bexleyheath in June 1944. It was originally a short wheelbase vehicle, but when it was re-bodied by Northern Coachbuilders in 1946 the chassis was lengthened, the vehicle re-numbered 98C and re-classified class D2C. It is seen here leaving Plumstead High Street and heading into Bostall Hill on route 698. The neat wiring on the left takes the 696 into Wickham Lane. *Denis Battams*

Numerically the last D3, No 553 is seen at Plumstead Station overtaking a more sedate form of transport. Griffin Road is on the right, and the reversing triangle wiring can clearly be seen. Here trolleybuses backed into Griffin Road, then turned right to travel back towards Bexleyheath. *Denis Battams*

Abbey Wood on 2nd March 1959. D2 class 399 has just turned short here and is parked on the loop wire. Wartime re-bodied 799B, class H1B, passes on the through wire on its way to Bexleyheath, its original body being destroyed in June 1944. The new one was constructed by East Lancs Coachbuilders in Blackburn and was one of an order of 25 placed with that company. Abbey Wood bus garage can be seen in the background. *Alan Cross*

An evocative night scene at Abbey Wood. 390B has just turned here, and will shortly be heading off back to Bexleyheath. It is early 1959, and on 3rd of March, the route will be replaced by buses. This trolleybus was re-bodied by East Lancs in October 1945 after bomb damage at Bexleyheath in June 1944. There is an ex-LCC tram shelter across the road in the background. *Alan Cross*

Another night view on route 698. 98C was re-bodied by Northern Coachbuilders and returned to London in March 1946 after damage in June 1944. In this case, the vehicle was originally a short wheelbase bus, and when it was re-bodied, the opportunity was taken to lengthen the chassis to the standard 30ft. It then became reclassified from class B2 to class D2C. *Alan Cross*

The trolleybuses on route 654 were fitted with coasting and run-back brakes for use on Anerley Hill. No 493 was from a second batch of five B1s delivered in September 1936, and is seen here on Anerley Hill. On descent, the driver would engage the brake before leaving the terminus at Crystal Palace, and it would not be disengaged until pole 24 was reached at the bottom of the hill. *Denis Battams*

The signage on the depot has been changed to read 'garage' denoting that electric traction here is almost at an end. An RT2 trainer is parked in the entrance with trolleybus staff looking on at what will soon be their new form of transport. In the meantime, B1 class trolleybus No 81 waits to proceed to Sutton on the 654 early in March 1959. *LTPS*

When the north London trams were being converted to trolleybuses in the late 1930s, a trial was carried out with a special trolleybus to operate through the Kingsway Subway. It was fitted with an offside loading platform to facilitate the central loading islands in the tunnel, but trolleybuses would have been difficult to negotiate through it. The vehicle built for this exercise was X5 class No 1379, an AEC/MCCW chassisless bus. When the idea was abandoned, the bus went to Holloway, where it worked until withdrawal in 1955. It stayed there in store for about a year before being sent for scrap. *Ronald Bristow*

This is Silvertown Station in 1959 with the Tate and Lyle sugar factory on the right. No 613 is an E2 class vehicle dating from 1937 and it is working from West Ham. It will turn short of its normal destination of Stratford Broadway, travelling around a clockwise loop at Plaistow, before returning to North Woolwich. On the left, a jellied eel cafe can be seen of the type long associated with east London. *John Wills*

Chadwell Heath Wangey Road was the terminus for trolleybus routes 693, 695 and bus route 86. The Mon-Sat 695 was another of the service cuts to be implemented on 7th January 1959. The 663 gave a partial replacement for it and Wangey Road also became the terminus of this route from January to August 1959. The route was shared between Bow and Ilford depots, and N1 class 1620 was from Bow. The vehicles turned inside Bow depot at the other end of the route, shown on the blinds as 'Bow Church'. *Peter Brazier*

Wood Green trolleybus 1262, of the K1 class, has just left the centre of Wood Green and heads north up High Road towards Green Lanes and Enfield on the 629. Potters Bar RT 304 is on the right and will share the same roads as far as Palmers Green, where it will head left into Alderman's Hill. Between the two vehicles can be seen a London Transport electrical substation. *Sid Hagerty*

It is 3rd August 1958 and C2 class No 208, delivered in June 1936, approaches Craven Park on route 664. Colindale depot has looked after the vehicle well, and it looks very smart in this view. It was one of the many C class buses fitted with rear wheel spats, which they retained until the end of their lives. The 664 was withdrawn in January 1959 ahead of the conversion of the routes from Colindale three years later. *Norman Rayfield*

This is Commercial Street at Gardiners Corner with K1 No 1133 on the left on route 647. The junction is wired for 647 route vehicles to travel straight across from north to south, and trolleybuses on routes 653, 661 and 663 to travel from east to west. At a more acute angle, and out of view on the right, is Commercial Road, where routes 567, 569 and 665 come in, with the 567 and 569 travelling to the left and the 665 heading north. *John Gillham*

This is Church Road, Leyton, with L3 class 1499 proceeding south towards Docks on the 687. The route was initially shared between West Ham and Walthamstow depots, but became exclusively a West Ham route in April 1944. It was withdrawn in April 1960. All of the buildings here still exist, although the Antelope pub is now closed. *C. Carter*

H1 class 780 was one of the last of its class to be withdrawn in July 1960 and is in Wandsworth High Street on route 630 working short to Mitcham. Towards the end of trolleybus operation, trolleybuses were the only vehicles permitted to turn right here. On the right is RTL 984, which carries a Metro-Cammell body. All of the buildings on the left have now been demolished. *Denis Battams*

Hammersmith, Queen Caroline Street, has now changed beyond recognition, the only remaining identifying reference point in this scene being St Paul's church, seen on the left. The Hammersmith flyover dominates this view now. F1 class 656 is out of service on the left, and is being passed by K1 No 1275 on its way to Harlesden on the 630. Maybe the passengers from 656 have just transferred, as both trolleybuses carry blinds for the northern terminus of the 630 - though those passengers not familiar with the route would hardly suspect this from the different ways of describing this point. The route would be replaced in July 1960. *Denis Battams*

A nice view of the complex overhead at Greengate. The main Barking Road is served by routes 567, 665 and 685. Route 699 came across the junction from left to right down Prince Regent Lane to the Docks. West Ham depot is situated off to the left. L3 class 1447 is followed by an RTW on the 15. *Denis Battams*

The impressive mass of crossovers and junctions in the overhead at The Bakers Arms, where routes 555, 557, 581, 661, 697 and 699 met. No 1349 is a K2 class vehicle operated by Lea Bridge depot. *John Clarke*

Some trolleybuses destined for South Africa during the war were diverted to London Transport, owing to the dangers of shipping being attacked. They were classified SA1, 2 and 3, and SA3 1757 is shown here. It was originally intended for Johannesburg, and had darkened glass windows fitted to guard against the South African sun! Note the decorations on the wall to the right of the vehicle, ready for the Coronation on 2nd June 1953. *John Smith*

1731 is from the SA1 class. Intended for Durban, the sealed off front door can be seen here along with the extra air vents above the lower saloon windows. It is in Ilford Lane just approaching Ilford High Road. The front axles were fitted with spacers to accommodate the 8ft width of these vehicles, but the rear ones were not, as is apparent here with the body overhanging the rear wheels. *Denis Battams*

This is the junction of Hampton Road with, on the left, Stanley Road. One of the second batch of Q1 trolleybuses, No 1857, is emerging on route 601, whilst on the right F1 class No 709 is working a Hanwell extra from Hampton Court to Brentford Half Acre. These extras occurred on Bank Holidays and ran between Hampton Court and Shepherds Bush, adding extra capacity to the regular 667. *Denis Battams*

This is Raynes Park, with the Southern Railway station visible on the embankment to the left. The Rialto cinema has unfortunately now gone. Q1 No 1797, from the first batch delivered in 1948, is en route for Wimbledon on the 605. It is showing the Sunday only blind, when the route was extended from Teddington to Twickenham. *Sid Hagerty*

A filthy night at Clapham Junction, and D2 class 464 is on route 628 bound for Harlesden, with a peak hour 626 following behind. The welcoming lights of the Express Dairy café beckon on the left. Adverts for the still very popular football pools adorn the front of the trolleybus, which is working from Hammersmith depot. *Alan Cross*

East Finchley Station was a short working used on routes 517, 609 and 617. N2 class 1667 stands on the forecourt of the station on a wet night on route 517, before returning to Holborn. This trolleybus spent its early life in the East End, before moving on to Highgate and Finchley. It ended its service days at Stonebridge, being finally withdrawn in January 1962. *Denis Battams*

Fortess Walk in Kentish Town. The white building on the far right, and the church in the background, are the only buildings still standing in this short link between Fortess Road and Highgate Road. NI No 1577 uses the wiring for its return to Highgate depot along Junction Road, after a duty on the 513. The N1 class began their life in east London at Bow depot, moving across London starting in the summer of 1958 and then after the third stage of the conversion programme in August 1959. *John Clarke*

28

Hampstead Heath terminus on a wet day in 1960. Routes 513, 613 and 639 shared this stand with buses on the 24 and 187. Trolleybus 1105 from the K1 class is from Highgate, and the conductor obviously feels it is dark enough to warrant having the saloon lights on. Trolleybuses ceased here after January 1961. *Sid Hagerty*

K1 class No 1274 passes through Manor House on route 629. The pub of the same name is on the left and was built in 1930 to replace an earlier structure. The building on the right houses the London Transport divisional offices, originally built by the Metropolitan Electric Tramways. It has today been converted into flats. The granite sets in the roadway have all since been removed, and the ground floor of the former pub is now a supermarket. *Sid Hagerty*

A view of Lea Bridge depot mid-1950s. Its main route was the 581, though there were a few very early journeys on the 555. The depot had been known as Leyton until the merger with Central Buses in 1950, when it was renamed to avoid confusion with the nearby Leyton bus garage. Three K2 class vehicles can be identified; 1344, 1337 and 1353. In the distance, a terminating 661 can be seen. The inspection pit shown here is dangerously unprotected, and maximum care would have to be taken to avoid mishaps! *J. L. Smith*

K2 class No 1221 was allocated to Stamford Hill depot and is busy on route 647. Balls Pond Road still has granite setts that replaced the tramlines at this point, and will be notoriously slippery for cyclists. The 25 minute journey between Stamford Hill and London Docks maintained a 5-minute headway on Mondays to Fridays. *Jack Gready*

H1 No 815 is turning right at Wood Green station for a return to the depot from route 625. Wood Green had a large allocation of the class before they were replaced with newer K class vehicles nearer to the end of operations. Wood Green shared this route with Walthamstow depot. *Denis Battams*

The lower saloon of trolleybus 97C, another vehicle re-bodied after war damage at Bexleyheath. This previously short-wheelbase vehicle was also lengthened to 30ft when the new body was fitted. The front nearside window has been lowered, no doubt so that the conductor can have a chat with the driver. *Alan Cross*

Hammersmith Grove on a wet day in the late 1950s. Four trolleybuses are lined up, three of which are on the outside wire for routes 660 and 666, which will travel back towards Acton. The second vehicle is a Q1 on the inner wire for route 667 en route for Hampton Court. The lead vehicle is C3 class 286 bound for North Finchley on the 660 and is an AEC with bodywork built by the Birmingham Railway Carriage and Wagon Company in 1936. *Fred Ivey*

Hanwell operated routes 607 and 655. The 607 was a main trunk route from Shepherds Bush to Uxbridge with a journey time of one hour and a frequency of between 2 and 5 minutes on Mondays to Fridays with a maximum vehicle requirement of 68 vehicles in 1960. F1 class No 747 is in Uxbridge passing the little used turning loop at the station. The wiring loop here was constructed in 1954, when road works prevented trolleybuses reaching their normal turning point.. *Denis Battams*

A nice line-up at Finsbury Park. On the 629 is 1074, a K1 from 1938, which is followed by L3 1529 on route 521. 1529 was one of six of the class fitted with sliding ventilators. Many people would have transferred to trolleybuses here from the very busy Finsbury Park station around the corner on the left. *Denis Battams*

Hammersmith Broadway is surrounded by building works for the new flyover, which would transform the area forever. On the left is Riverside bus garage. The line-up of vehicles are a Lyons Albion articulated lorry, K1 class trolleybus 1083 on route 628, and AEC tower wagon 1073Q. The tower wagon was one of five supplied in 1958 to help with the dismantling of the system. The local authority is using the traction standards to support the street lighting. *Denis Battams*

The F1 class were the mainstay at Hanwell depot for many years. They were an-all Leyland product, and proved to be very reliable. The main 607 route from Shepherds Bush to Uxbridge was their domain, and good speeds were attained on the open roads beyond Southall. No 665 is passing the depot in this scene on a sunny day early in 1960; it would all change in November when the vehicle and the route would be withdrawn. *Norman Rayfield*

Hackney on a grey day in 1958. Two K1 class trolleybuses, 1298 and 1150, approach the junction with 1298 about to turn right on the 677 and 1150 taking the inner wire to turn left on its way to Woodford on the 581. A Ford Consul obscures the identity of the other K class vehicle working short to Islington Green. Both routes would cease to operate in April 1959, when Clapton depot would be converted to buses, and Lea Bridge closed. *Denis Battams*

A short turn existed at New North Road, Baring Street, being most frequently used by routes 611 and 641. Trolleybuses from classes J1 and L1 were used on the 611, and were fitted with coasting and run-back brakes for use on Highgate Hill. L1 1355 is seen here in Baring Street about to turn right as the conductor pulls the frog. RTW 104 has also turned short here on the 76 before returning to Tottenham garage. *John Clarke*

L3 class 1445 has just travelled down Junction Road from Highgate depot, and turned right into Fortess Walk, where it will turn right again to take up duties on the 615.
An Inspector ensures all is well. Junction Road, between here and the depot, was not served by a trolleybus route, but members of the public were allowed to use the service when vehicles were running to and from the depot. This point was also used as a short working, although buses were not allowed to stand here due to the proximity of the Fire Station, seen on the left of the vehicle. *Denis Battams*

An animated scene at Clapham Junction. On the left is F1 class No 702 that will shortly terminate, its blind already having been set for the return to Hanwell on the 655. In the centre is P1 class 1703 on route 626 with RTL 1194 on route 19 coming through on the inside. The P1 class were delivered during the war in 1940 and 1941. The car following 702 is unusual. It has a late 1950s fibreglass body, probably a Fairlight on a 1939 Ford 10hp chassis. The Fairlight firm evolved to become supercar maker Ginetta. *Denis Battams*

This is the junction of Blackhorse Road with Forest Road in Walthamstow. Routes 685 and 687 proceeded straight across here, whilst the 623 and 625 used the through wires from left to right. E1 class No 587 has a full load on the 687, as it negotiates the crossroads on its way to Crooked Billet. The vehicle is nearing the end of its life; it will be withdrawn in February 1960, and the route in April. *Norman Rayfield*

Green Lanes on a wet day in late autumn 1961 and K2 1246 is approaching the Water Works just before Manor House. The bus stop flag has been moved from the traction pole on which a 'yellow peril' notice can be seen, indicating that trolleybuses on this route and from Wood Green depot will shortly cease. This trolleybus was damaged at Hackney in September 1940 and was rebuilt with a much flatter roof than the rest of the class. *Terry Cooper Collection/Mick Webber*

Route 677 worked from Smithfield to West India Docks, and was operated by Clapton depot. K1 class 1123 was re-numbered 1123A after being re-bodied by Weymann in December 1941. Its body had been destroyed by enemy action in November 1940. It turns into West India Dock Road early in 1959, and the route was withdrawn in April of that year. *Denis Battams*

Hammersmith's K2 1176 turns into King Street at Acton Market Place and is ready for its return trip to Clapham Junction from here on the 626, a Mon-Fri peak hour route. Recruitment posters grace the front of the vehicle, a sign of the shortage of bus crews and also commercial advertising at this time. *Denis Battams*

The Kingsland Road was a very busy trolleybus thoroughfare and here we see five vehicles proceeding south on routes 647, 649 and 543. The trolleybuses are all K types, with K1 1152 in front, followed by K3 1696, and K2 1213 at the rear. The K1 and K2 batches were delivered in 1938 and 1939, and the K3s arrived late in 1940. The drivers would all have remembered to take their foot off of the power as they pass beneath the power feeder. *Denis Battams*

Stamford Hill. K2 class 1206 is turning right to return to the depot in this 1961 view. It has travelled up from London Docks on the 647. Tottenham RTL 601 is also returning home on the 73 from its cross London journey from Richmond. The future, in the shape of a new Routemaster, lurks in the background. *Denis Battams*

Shoreditch Church in the early 1960s, and K1 1131 from Stamford Hill depot turns right into Old Street, whilst RTW 195 turns into Hackney Road on the 6. The 543 and 643 operated a loop at Holborn Circus, the 543 anti-clockwise, and the 643 clockwise. Both routes were converted in July 1961. A typical corner shop tobacconist and confectioner of the time is seen on the left. *Denis Battams*

This is the junction of Whitechapel High Street, from left to right, and Commercial Street to the north, with Leman Street to the south. The other routes at this point have all now been withdrawn, leaving just the 647 to linger until July 1961. 1206 and 1221 are both K2 class vehicles delivered in November 1938 and December 1939 respectively. Public toilets under road junctions were still commonplace at this time, as can be seen here on the traffic island, where a motor-cycle and sidecar have been parked. *Denis Battams*

This is The Bell junction at Walthamstow, a favourite for trolleybus photographers with its impressive overhead. We are looking down Chingford Road, and routes 557, 697 and 699 came through here and straight across into Hoe street for the centre of the town. Routes 623 and 625 crossed the junction from left to right. The curves to the left are for depot journeys, Walthamstow depot being a few hundred yards down Chingford Road. The vehicle is H1 class No 884. *John Clarke*

The very complex junction at Ilford Broadway can be seen here. Routes 691 and 693 emerged from the right, with the 691 proceeding straight across and the 693 turning right. The main trunk route 663 worked straight through between Chadwell Heath and Aldgate. N1 class 1573 from Bow heads towards the camera in this late 1950s view. *John Clarke*

Seven Sisters Road, approaching the Nags Head. The crew of tower wagon 83Q are attending to the points where trolleybuses on routes 521, 621, 659 and 679 will take the inner wire to turn left. K2 No 1313 takes the centre wire to work straight on to Tottenham Court Road on the 629. The bus stop shows that the 653 has already been replaced by bus 253 at this time, which dates this view between February and April 1961. *Denis Battams*

A short turn was provided at City Road, Windsor Terrace in March 1938. No points were provided here, and the conductor had to execute a pole swap to the terminal wire. The conductor waits for the driver to complete his manoeuvre before replacing the bamboo pole back in its tube under the vehicle. 1466 is an L3 class bus based at Finchley.
Denis Battams

The short turn at Holloway Nags Head involved a loop via Camden Road and Warlters Road. M1 class trolleybus 1544 is in Warlters Road, where these large vehicles looked rather out of place on route 609, having just passed a trolleybus sub-station. The M1 class were delivered early in the war in 1939. *Denis Battams*

This is Chingford Mount terminus on 9th August 1959. Routes 557, 697 and 699 all turned here, and L3 No 1400 waits on the 697 for a return trip to the Docks. A bamboo pole hangs on the traction standard on the left to assist in any pole movements that may be necessary. Francis Durbridge was one of the leading crime writers of his day, his work often being adapted for television. *Norman Rayfield*

Jolly Butchers Hill in Wood Green. K1 No 1291 is about to turn left into Wood Green depot after running in from the 627, on which Wood Green had a small allocation. It is a dreary wet day in 1961, and the dome of the local library dominates the background. The local style street lights were fitted to the traction standards in this area, as can be seen behind the vehicle, where the feeder cables are also visible. *Sid Hagerty*

The long trunk route 607 between Uxbridge and Shepherds Bush was ideal for the Q1 class vehicles, with plenty of dual carriageway in the outer suburbs. 1851 from the 1952 batch passes the Askew Arms junction, where routes 660 and 666 leave and join the Uxbridge Road to and from Hammersmith. This vehicle was to see further service in Bilbao in Spain in 1961. 125 of the 127 Q1s were sold to Spanish operators in 1961. *Denis Battams*

Colindale trolleybus N1 class No 1583 has taken the wire to turn right from Cricklewood Lane into the Edgware Road towards Canons Park on the 645. In the background, another N1 prepares to take the inner wire to travel across the Broadway to Chichele Road on its way to Hammersmith on the 660. These N1 class vehicles had been transferred across London from Bow after the conversion there in August 1959. *Denis Battams*

K1 1255 and K3 1674 pass on routes 543 and 649. The Edmonton vehicle on the 649 will be turning short at Dalston. This main thoroughfare of Kingsland Road and Stoke Newington High Street was a trolleybus stronghold, the RTW on the 76 being the only bus route at this point. *Denis Battams*

The turn at Finsbury Park involved an anti-clockwise loop via Coleridge Road and Isledon Road behind the Astoria cinema. The route most frequently using this stand was the 653, but in this view, Finchley's L3 class 1456 is seen on the 621. Routes 653 and 629 have already been replaced as can be seen by the Routemasters behind on new routes 253 and 269. RM 684 is an Edmonton bus that worked the route between April and October 1961. *Fred Ivey*

L2 class 954 was the forerunner of a larger batch of chassisless vehicles built by AEC and MCCW. It was immediately recognisable by the extension of the cream band around the front of the vehicle. It operated mainly from Highgate depot, but was later transferred to Finchley. It passes Theobalds Road on its way along Grays Inn Road in company with RTL 879, which also has MCCW bodywork. *Fred Ivey*

Route 685 operated from Walthamstow, Crooked Billet to Canning Town, with some journeys extended to Silvertown and North Woolwich. There was, however, a service which worked from Crooked Billet to Lea Bridge Road in Saturday shopping hours, turning via a loop in Waterloo Road and Gloucester Road. E2 class 617 has just left that loop and is turning from Lea Bridge Road into Markhouse Road. A special 'lazy' blind was used for this working. *Fred Ivey*

Two K2 trolleybuses, the leading vehicle being 1305, occupy the stand at Clerkenwell Green in early 1959. Route 555 will be withdrawn in April. Immediately behind the second vehicle is the Farringdon tower wagon shed which, at the time of writing, still exists. A trolleybus passes by in the distance in Farringdon Road. Both vehicles are running back to Leyton, Downsell Road. *Denis Battams*

Red Lion Square, Bloomsbury, was the terminus for routes 555, 581 and 665. Clapton K2 No 1240 leaves on the 555, with Poplar L3 1471 following behind on a short working 665 to East Ham. The 555 is working a rush hour extension of the route beyond Leyton Green to Downsell Road. *Fred Ivey*

K2 class 1354 from Lea Bridge stands outside the Everyman's Library in Parton Street, around the corner from the previous view. Bowstring brackets were employed here. The 665 day and night services also used this stand. After withdrawal of services in November 1959, Parton Street was closed, and the site built on. *Norman Rayfield*

Two Clapton K types in Clerkenwell Road on 2nd April 1959. 1252 on the left, is a K2 on route 555, and about to turn left towards Smithfield, is K1 1259 on the 677, The two K classes differed only in the makers of their control equipment, the K1s having Metrovick and the K2s English Electric. *Denis Battams*

Green Street, West Ham. The Stratford circular routes 689 and 690 passed here with the 689 working the clockwise service and the 690 anti-clockwise. L3 1499 on the 690 is about to turn left into Barking Road, whilst sister L3 1505 turns right on the 685 to Canning Town. The merchant's shop on the left sells a very varied selection of goods! *John Clarke*

The traction standard bearing the frog pull from Warlters Road to Parkhurst Road, was set back on private ground, and therefore had to be cantilevered out over the boundary wall. The conductor operates the frog for N1 class 1566, as it turns left. It is working short to Mornington Crescent Station on the 627. *Fred Ivey*

Route 691 was normally the domain of the SA class trolleybuses, but Bow loaned extra vehicles on Saturdays to meet the increased requirements, and N1 class 1579 illustrates an example of this. The Charlton produced destination blind includes a rare use of an ampersand and refers to the route's northern terminus at the top of Barkingside High Street a quarter of a mile from Fairlop station. The gent's tailor Weaver to Wearer in Ilford Broadway has long since vanished from our streets. *Fred Ivey*

This is Plaistow High Street, with Walthamstow K1 No 1283 on its way to Chingford Mount on the 699. A 687 prepares to pull out of Clegg Street on the left. Stone setts are still the preferred road surface here, and parked at the kerb is one of the once familiar newspaper delivery vans, in this case advertising 'The Star', a London evening paper which ceased publication in 1960. *Fred Ivey*

L3 class 1448 on route 567, is approaching the junction at Greengate in West Ham. The wires off to the right will take the 699 past West Ham depot on its way to Chingford Mount, with the wires to the left leading to the Docks.
John Clarke

This is Lea Bridge Road, and K1 1290 is passing the wires into and out of Lea Bridge depot, which it is about to pass. The London Master Bakers arch and building on the right remain.
John Clarke

K2 No 1229 has worked the 683 from Moorgate to Stamford Hill. After dropping off passengers, it prepares to run in to Stamford Hill depot. The route was a casualty of the service cuts made on 6th January 1959, a couple of months before the trolleybus route conversion programme got under way. The route operated on Monday to Saturday only and had started in February 1939. *Lyndon Rowe*

Route 567 worked from Barking to Aldgate, but certain journeys were diverted from Aldgate to run via Commercial Street and Clerkenwell to Smithfield. N1 class 1597 is on one of those journeys, returning from Smithfield, and is seen in Commercial Street on its way to Barking, with the British Railways Bishopsgate goods building behind. *Fred Ivey*

Woodstock Street provided a stand for vehicles turning at Canning Town, and bowstring bracket arms provided the support for the wires. Route 685 towards Crooked Billet, started here, and Walthamstow K1 No 1103 looking very smart, waits time, with an N2 class vehicle behind. Some wartime Nissen huts, named after Major Peter Nissen the inventor, can be seen on the right. *Denis Battams*

On a wet night at Finsbury Square, the bus stop flag shows the routes that terminated here before inroads were made in the conversion scheme. The Q plate at the bottom asks passengers to queue the relevant side for trolleybuses travelling up City Road or New North Road. The enamel E plates would be highly sought after in today's collectors market. *Alan Cross*

Green Lanes, approaching Manor House. Holloway RT 1303 changes crew on the 171, whilst K1 No 1277 passes on a 641 short working to Baring Street. Behind is 1472, one of the L3 class with sliding ventilators, followed by a new Routemaster on the 629 replacement route 269. Wood Green operated trolleybuses and buses at this stage of the conversion programme. *Tony Belton*

The Baring Street, New North Road short working was frequently used by trolleybuses on the 641. Wood Green vehicle K2 No 1323 makes the turn from the north, with the Regents Canal behind the wall on the right. *Fred Ivey*

The bridge over the railway in Scrubs Lane remains intact, minus the troughing for the trolleybus wires. Today, though, the scene would be somewhat busier. K1 No 1122 from Hammersmith depot is on its way to West Croydon on the 630 in this 1960 view. *Norman Rayfield*

Routes 627, 649, 659 and 679 all reached Waltham Cross, the most northerly point for London trolleybuses. Edmonton's P1 class No 1718 was a wartime 1941 delivery, and has made the left turn into the main Hertford Road to head south on a scheduled short working 659 to Finsbury Park Station. It is 6th September 1959. *Norman Rayfield*

The turn at Liverpool Street was one of the tightest on the system, and was used by the 557, 649 and 649A. Two turning wires were provided here, the farthest one being the most used. K2 class 1213 prepares to turn on Sunday only route 649A, and waits for RTW 39 to pass on the 8B, whilst a K3 on the 649 queues in the background. *Tony Belton*

Holborn Circus, with Prince Albert prominent. The Daily Mirror building had only recently been completed in 1961 when this photograph was taken, but lasted only until 1994. K1 class 1135 navigates the statue on a Sunday, a day that was very much quieter in those more measured times. *Terry Cooper Collection*

The Docks terminus had an intense service on routes 687, 697 and 699, with trolleybuses from West Ham and Walthamstow depots. E2 class 607 has just left the stand on its way to Crooked Billet, and J2 974 and K1 1058 will edge forward and enter the turning circle on the left. The Silvertown and North Woolwich railway line is on the right. *John Wills*

Park Royal bodied N2 1646 from Stonebridge waits at the last stop in Cricklewood Lane before the Broadway. A frog pull is situated on the pole on the right, where the outer wire will take 645s to the right up Edgware Road and the inner wire is straight on for 660s to Chichele Road. Feeder wires are located one pole back. *Norman Rayfield*

This is the Holloway Road, just south of the Nags Head junction. The L3 is 1460 from Finchley on route 609, and it is followed by a Metro-Cammell bodied RTL on the 172 and new RM 591 on route 271, which had just replaced trolleybus route 611. The 609 and 271 will soon split with the 609 traversing Upper Street and City Road, and the 271 going down New North Road. They will meet again at Old Street, and then share the road to Moorgate. *Tony Belton*

The turning facility at Turnpike Lane Underground Station, was frequently used by trolleybuses on route 641. Two K1s, 1302 and 1294, are in this view and will work south to Moorgate. The three buses in view are RT 1623 on the 144, RTL 1576 on the 29, and RTL 1423 on the 29A.
Tony Belton

The Springfield Park Tavern and adjoining buildings are still all *in situ* in Bounds Green Road. Finchley L3 1497 leaves the request stop here on route to North Finchley early in 1961 and the journey time back to Holborn is scheduled at 52 minutes. The route had served the area since March 1938.
Sid Hagerty

The 649A was a Sunday only route from Wood Green to Liverpool Street Station operated by Stamford Hill and the only post-war route to have a letter suffix. K1 No 1112 is in Lordship Lane at Wood Green and will shortly turn left to enter the anti-clockwise turning loop to stand in Redvers Road. The outer wire here was for trolleybuses to turn right for Wood Green depot and Winchmore Hill. *Terry Cooper Collection/Mick Webber*

Routes in the 600 series worked a clockwise loop at Holborn, and K2 No 1213, from Stamford Hill enters Charterhouse Street from Farringdon Road on route 643. It will return via Grays Inn Road toward Kings Cross. It was a fifty minute journey from Wood Green, requiring a maximum of thirty vehicles. *Terry Cooper Collection/Mick Webber*

Trouble at the top of Ilford Hill. N1 class 1574 from Bow has dewired at the junction on route 663 and an Inspector gets involved in trying to resolve the situation.
The driver is on his way from the terminus at Thorold Road. The junction here was one of the most complex on the system. The driver of the 1947 Thames van turns his head.
Robin Newell Collection

D2 class 452 is a Hammersmith vehicle seen around the corner from the place where its depot is situated. Overhead 'fairy lights' can be seen between the wires, used to guide drivers in bad weather. Pole 142 on the left has a white band painted on it to warn drivers to take their foot off of the power when passing under the feeder cables. *Fred Ivey*

The Triangle at Wembley was wired up to take short workings and extras working along the Harrow Road for Wembley Stadium events. Three vehicles are leaving the circle and re-joining the main road, with C3 class 354 in the lead. The 662 passed through here from Paddington to the right, and on to Sudbury to the left. In addition to the stadium extras, some scheduled turns also took place here. *John Clarke*

Goldhawk Road, 2nd January 1962. The through wires are for route 657 and the trolleybuses in view are turning out of Askew Road on the left and into Paddenswick Road on the right. Routes 660 and 666 followed this path, and two unidentified N1s take the centre wire, which is guided by 'fairy lights'. *John Gillham*

Craven Park junction. The routes here ceased on 2nd January 1962, and this view on that day shows N1 1632 running in to Stonebridge depot on the 660. It has just turned right from the main route and will use the 662 wires, which run straight through at this point, to run in. Route 666 also used this junction, sharing the same wires as the 660. *John Gillham*

N1 class 1573 is a Colindale vehicle on route 666 at Harlesden Jubilee Clock in the last days for routes at stage 13 of the conversion scheme. It approaches the junction in the High Street, and will turn right here for Hammersmith, a path it shared with the 626 and 660. The 662 turned left here. Routes 626, 628 and 664 also used this junction, but had been withdrawn by this time. *Fred Ivey*

It is New Year's Eve 1961, and N1 class Colindale trolleybus 1570 stands silent in the snow at St Gabriel's Church on route 645. Trolleybuses had to leave their line of route on this service, to turn here, and would travel the short distance down Chichele Road from Cricklewood Broadway before turning into Walm Lane. *Denis Battams*

L3 No 1521 had been carefully prepared on 8th May 1962 for the final run of a London trolleybus that evening on route 604. Special posters had been applied, and balloons with streamers tied to the booms. It stands in the yard at Fulwell depot awaiting departure for Hampton Court. Soon it will be on its way to Wimbledon with a procession of cars and motorcycles following behind. The author was on board, and a memorable occasion it was too. George Cohen saved the vehicle from scrap and it was presented to the Historical Commercial Vehicle Club. It now runs at the East Anglia Transport Museum in Suffolk. *Terry Cooper*

The fate for most of London trolleybuses. This is Bird's yard at Stratford upon Avon. The company scrapped a large number of vehicles between March 1956 and September 1958, but lost out to Cohen's when the main contract was awarded. C2 class No 256 is left of centre in this view taken in May 1956.